A Little Adventure

Story by Jenny Giles
Illustrations by Genevieve Rees

NELSON PRICE MILBURN

Abby sat on the steps with her friends from next door.

"I wish we could go hiking like Nick," she said, as she watched her brother leaving with his camping gear.

"That would be fun!" said Lucy.

Caitlin looked at her sister. "But our parents would never let us," she said, gloomily.

Abby jumped to her feet. "Just a minute — I know where we could go hiking!" she said. "My aunt and uncle have got a track that goes through some bush on their farm. Nick and I rode our bikes along it last holidays."

"Well…" said Abby's father, when the girls asked him, "I don't see why not. You'd be quite safe there. Why don't you phone Aunty Kath and ask her?"

Abby ran inside, and her friends followed.

"Aunty Kath says we can come tomorrow!" Abby said. "Let's go and ask your parents now."

The girls' parents agreed to let them go, and helped to make a list of the things they would need.

"After the hike, we'll be able to have a ride on the flying fox that I was telling you about," said Abby. "You'll love it."

"Fantastic!" said Caitlin.

"It'll be really **exciting**!" said Lucy.

5

When they arrived at the farm, the girls put on their backpacks.

"Take our mobile phone with you," said Aunty Kath, "so that you can call us if you need to."

They all waved to Abby's father as they walked towards the trees. "Remember to stay on the track," he told them. "I'll meet you at the other end."

"This is going to be fun!" shouted Lucy, and she started to run.

"Hey! Slow down!" called Caitlin. "We have to stay with Abby, because she's the one who knows the way."

The three girls set off together. It was quiet and cool in the bush, and they looked up at the tall trees as they went along.

"I like hiking," said Caitlin, "and it's fun being out here by ourselves."

"It's a little adventure!" said Abby.

After a while, they stopped to have a drink and a banana each.

Lucy dropped her banana skin beside a tree. "Don't do that," said her sister. "You mustn't leave rubbish in the bush."

"Fruit is all right," said Abby, "because things like banana skins are food for the trees."

"Then I'm feeding this tree," said Lucy.

"I'll feed it, too," said Abby.

"And so will I," laughed Caitlin. "Now come on, or we'll never finish our hike."

The girls went on and on along the track. "We must be nearly there," said Abby, as they reached a bend.

Just then, they heard an unusual bird call. Clear musical notes were coming from somewhere in the trees behind them.

"Listen to that bird," cried Lucy. "I'm going to find it!" And she ran off into the bush.

"Come back, Lucy!" called Abby. "The bird will just fly away when it hears you coming!"

Caitlin rushed after Lucy, and caught up to her.

Abby followed them. "Come back, you two," she shouted, "or we'll all get lost!"

"Sorry," said Lucy. "I just wanted to see what the bird looked like."

"But now we don't know where the track is!" said Caitlin, crossly.

"I can see it," said Abby. "Come with me."

The girls found the track, and continued with their hike. After a while, Abby said, "We should be there by now." She sounded puzzled; it was taking much longer than she'd expected.

Suddenly Lucy stopped and pointed at the ground. "Oh, no!" she groaned. "Look down here."

Right beside the track were their three banana skins.

The girls stared at each other in dismay.

"We've been going the wrong way!" said Abby. "We've walked all the way back to this tree. How did we manage to do that?"

"It must have happened when Lucy ran into the bush to see that bird," said Caitlin.

"Yes," said Abby, "and when we found the track again, we got muddled."

"What can we do?" asked Lucy. "My legs are tired."

"We could phone Abby's dad," said Caitlin, "but we'd never be allowed to go hiking by ourselves again."

"And we'd never hear the end of it from Nick," said Abby, gloomily.

"Come on!" said Caitlin. "We can finish the hike! We'll eat some chocolate while we're walking."

The others cheered up. They all had a drink, and then nibbled their chocolate as they walked back the way they had come.

The track seemed to be endless, and just when they were thinking that they couldn't take another step, they saw sunshine breaking through the trees.

"We're there!" cried Abby.

The girls forgot about their aching legs, and ran to where Abby's dad was waiting for them.

"You've been rather a long time," he said. "I was beginning to think you were lost."

The girls grinned at each other.

"We weren't really lost," said Abby. "We just had a little adventure."